Living Things Need
Air

by Karen Aleo

PEBBLE
a capstone imprint

Little Pebble is published by Pebble
1710 Roe Crest Drive, North Mankato, Minnesota 56003
www.mycapstone.com

Library of Congress Cataloging-in-Publication Data
Names: Aleo, Karen, author.
Title: Living things need air / by Karen Aleo.
Description: North Mankato, Minnesota : Pebble, [2019] | Series: Little
Pebble. What living things need | "Pebble is published by Capstone." |
Audience: Ages 5-7. | Audience: K to grade 3.
Identifiers: LCCN 2019006174| ISBN 9781977108845 (hardcover) | ISBN
9781977110343 (pbk.) | ISBN 9781977108883 (ebook pdf)
Subjects: LCSH: Life (Biology)--Juvenile literature. | Biochemistry--Juvenile
literature. | Air--Juvenile literature. | Respiration--Juvenile literature.
Classification: LCC QH309.2 .A44 2019 | DDC 572--dc23
LC record available at https://lccn.loc.gov/2019006174

Editorial Credits
Anna Butzer, editor; Bobbie Nuytten, designer;
Kelly Garvin, media researcher; Kathy McColley, production specialist

Photo Credits
Shutterstock: A.Hixon, 21, amenic181, 15, Felix Mizioznikov, 5, greenland, 17, hanapon1002, 11,
Mark Bridger, 9, Osetrik, 13, Rawpixel.com, 19, S Curtis, 7, Tuzemka, cover

All internet sites appearing in back matter were available and accurate when this book was sent
to press.

Printed and bound in China.
1671

Table of Contents

Air All Around. 4

Air Is a Need. 8

Keeping Air Clean 16

Glossary 22
Read More 23
Internet Sites. 23
Critical Thinking Questions. 24
Index 24

Air All Around

Breathe in.

You are taking in air.

Air is all around.

You can feel it as wind.

Whoosh!

Air Is a Need

Living things need air.

It helps them stay alive.

Gases make up air.

Oxygen is a gas in air.

Animals need oxygen.
It helps their organs
work right.

Carbon dioxide is

a gas in air.

Plants use it to make food.

Keeping Air Clean

We can help keep
the air clean.
We ride our bikes
to school.

Reducing waste
can help too.

We can recycle.

All living things need air.

Let's keep it clean.

Glossary

breathe—to take air in and out of the lungs

carbon dioxide—a gas that has no smell or color

gas—something that is not solid or liquid and does not have a shape

need—to require something; you need food, shelter, and air to stay alive

organ—a body part that does a certain job

oxygen—a colorless gas that people and animals breathe; people and animals need oxygen to live

wind—moving air

Read More

Andersen, Jill. *We Need Air to Breathe*. Rosen Real Readers: Stem and Steam Collection. New York: Rosen Publishing, 2017.

Brett, Flora. *Your Respiratory System Works!* Your Body Systems. North Mankato, MN.: Capstone Press, 2015.

Rivera, Andrea. *Air*. Zoom in on Science Concepts. Minneapolis: Abdo Zoom, 2018.

Internet Sites

NASA: Climate Kid—10 Interesting Things about Air
https://climatekids.nasa.gov/10-things-air/

Kids Biology: Oxygen
https://kidsbiology.com/biology-basics/air-oxygen/

Santa Barbara County Air Pollution Control District: What Kids Can Do to Help Clean Our Air
https://www.ourair.org/wp-content/uploads/facts-kids.pdf

Critical Thinking Questions

1. Why do living things need air?

2. How do plants take in air? How do people and animals use air?

3. How can you help keep the air clean?

Index

animals, 12

breathing, 4

carbon dioxide, 14

food, 14

oxygen, 10, 12

plants, 14

recycling, 18

wind, 6